Purposeful Pain

LATEEHAH LINTON

Purposeful Pain

TRM Publications

a division of TRM Enterprises, LLC

Cover designed by Gifted Dezyns Graphics Firm, LLC

DEDICATION

I give honor and glory to God for allowing me to write this book for ordering my words and for putting the right people around me to push me to write.

I dedicate this book to my beautiful five children: Tymier, Tyjeim, Taivier, Tanaiyah, and Lailah. I could not have asked for such a wonderful bunch of children. We have had ups and downs, and we still keep moving. I love you all for always pushing me, believing in me, desiring to be like me, for trusting the God in me to guide you the right way. Most importantly I love you for knowing that God is our source and that we will always be victorious no matter what comes our way!

To my beautiful mother who has always had my back and made sacrifices in her life to make sure that I have the best. My ride or die. Love you forever

To my big brother Michael love you to the moon and back for the many years of pushing me to be better.

To my sister in law Mary, Girl you are my ride or die, and I love you to the moon and back! Thank you for always being there for me and for talking me down off the ledge at times. (inside joke) you are a true prayer warrior.

ACKNOWLEDGEMENT

To My Pastor Dier Hopkins, Next Level Thinking, and the New Direction Family:

Words cannot express my gratitude for all the selfless acts you have done for me and my family. Pastor Hopkins, for your many days of encouraging me, pushing me, correcting me, stabilizing me and showing me that there is much greater in me than on the surface. Thank you for not giving up on me and not walking away from me when I didn't want to be corrected or when I didn't want to deal with the things that hurt me and tried to hinder me. Thank you for embracing me in a time that I felt like I was alone. I will be forever grateful to you.

To Dr. Deitra Hill:

Oh my God, I know that without a shadow of a doubt that God connected us together and this divine connection will never be broken. You have prayed for me, inspired me and pushed me to be better. You spoke life into me when I thought I was going to die. You cried with me, and you held on to me. You took me to another level of believing in

God and the things that were trying to kill me. You are an awesome woman of God, and I bless God for you. I thank you for standing in the gap for me and not letting me go. Thank you for also believing in me and reassuring me that "All is well," I love you!

To Dr. T.L. Penny:

I walked in your church at the time of my life where all hell broke loose, and you stood in front of me and said "MAKE Pain Pay for what happened to you "and then your next statement was "write a book or a blog." Because God used you to speak to me, this book was produced, thank you!

To Bishop Marc L House:

Thank you for the years that you poured into me and for allowing me to grow and to have a real relationship with God. Thank you for teaching me that I can have a relationship with God that is more real than people, air and the things of this world.

Last but not least, none of this would be possible without this quiet Giant none other than, Tachina Mack!

Girl, you have taken me and my dreams and pushed me inspired me and kept me moving. You prayed with me, cried with me and pushed me. Because of your belief in me, that's why this is possible. I could have never asked God to set me up with a better person to do business with you are so self- less. You have broadened my horizon with knowledge and favor and I thank you so much. You shared so much with me and have given me "golden nuggets" to remember, and I will never forget what you have instilled in me. I pray God's continual blessings in your life, love you!

Dionne Coleman:
Thank you for believing in me and for pushing me and for listening to Tachina about me. Thank you for your words of wisdom and encouragement.

Contents:

INTRODUCTION

This book was written to reach the individuals that have gone through many obstacles in life and have a desire to be healed and move forward. In each topic, you will be able to identify and see yourself and prayerfully you will begin to make the necessary changes in your life to move forward and walk in your purpose.

PREVIEW PAGE

The war in your members comes from your flesh fighting the spirit man. God is trying to take you to another level, but you keep fighting the spirit and walking in the flesh. There has been trouble on both sides of you, all around you, people walked away from you only because God was trying to show you what he couldn't show to anyone else that is YOU. Now let's begin...

CHAPTER 1
FRUSTRATION

I was in a place where everything in my life

seemed to have been closing in on me. My job had at a

place where I could not be challenged. The owner would

make up rules and do various things toward me to try to

get me to second guess myself. I began to realize that

the job was not where I was supposed to be because

God had already given me vision as to where I needed to

begin to work for myself. In the meantime the monthly

bonuses I was supposed to have received was not given

to me on a monthly basis but whenever the owner felt

like I should have received one. Six month evaluation

changed from receiving it in six months to quarterly.

 My place of living was too small. I hated coming

home to where I lived because it felt like the walls

were closing in on me and I could never have my

own place of privacy. So what happened?

I got frustrated because God had already given me the solution to my issues. He showed me everything I needed to do. He gave me gifts and talents, and I knew what they were, but I never stepped out totally or fully relying on God. So with the job I made the owner over $80,000.00 the first month and instead of me receiving the bonus that we had agreed upon when I got hired he kept changing the guidelines. That's when I realized it was time for me to begin to put my faith to work and work for myself. When you realize who you are what you possess, you get frustrated because you're stuck in a place where no one wants to recognize who you are or even pay you what you are worth. I sat at my desk telling myself you have to start your businesses. You have to find someone to help you get started. You have to leave this place and form your own company, your own legacy, your own dynasty.

I decided to look at the situation with my spiritual eye. God gave me a multi-million dollar business idea. The more I didn't do the work that God called me to do the more I was being disobedient, and God would continue to allow things to frustrate me because I was not operating in my purpose.

"For I know the thoughts that I think toward you, says the Lord, thoughts of peace and not of evil, to give you a future and a hope". Jeremiah 29:11 (NKJV)

We don't realize that God has already established a place for us to end up and to arrive. He has formed our ending before our beginning. He knew when he gave us the business idea, the desire to work in certain place, the desire to own companies, write books, and buy homes what we were going to go through in order for it to all work.

The problem Is when we are in a place where God is trying to push us into better, greater we begin to get frustrated because we get complacent in areas that God told us years prior to moving forward. So because we won't move, he allows things to happen to make us move. So you get frustrated because you're on a job barely making ends meet, you're in relationships that are meaningless, you're around people that drain you and take from you, and you get nothing in return.

So by the time you get a chance to get alone to focus on what you're supposed to be working on you're too frustrated to focus.

The frustration is the attitude, aggravation the annoyance from everything that's around you that is hindering you. You're frustrated because you're not operating in the gift, the anointing, and the capacity that God has given you to access or walk in. You're not walking in your purpose.

It's like a professional swimmer swimming in a kiddy pool when he is supposed to be swimming in an

Olympic pool doing laps. No matter how he keeps trying to swim in the kiddie pool, all he does is hit his knees on the bottom of the pool. He hasn't realized that he's out grown the kiddie pool and can swim freely in the Olympic size pool. That's because he has allowed situation to frustrate him and temporary cripple him and blind him in believing he has to remain in a place that he is no longer able to fit in, that which he has out grown.

Whatever you do when you become frustrated with your life, get back to the place where you got the release... If that means go for a walk, exercise, laugh more, do it so you can get to your place of destiny. Surround yourself with people that will push you, motivate you, believe in you and push you to take steps to your future.

CHAPTER 2
LOVE

We are born into this world wanting to be love and expecting love but what we never get told is that everyone isn't going to love us the way that we deserve to be loved or even love us just of who we are. What many people fail to realize is who they are the value that they hold and possess?

Love is an intense feeling of deep affection....There are times as your growing in life you are desiring that feeling. You're going to want to be loved or what to love someone else... The problem is more than likely when we are at that vulnerable state that we tend to fall in love with the wrong person. Reason being is because we are so eager to be in a relationship with someone else that we have not or do not take the time to love ourselves or even find out what we would know to be love..

More often we get trapped into situations that we call love at the worst time of our lives. Normally, it's when we just came out of some life changing disaster. The death of a loved one, location move, or even a breakup. Because one of these things has happened there is now a door that has opened you up to be susceptible to anyone that appears to love you but they don't. They prey on you and where you are at that time of your life. So they may come camouflaged as something that they really aren't. They may mask as a friend, someone that really cares about you, someone that wants to be by your side, a pastor, a sister, brother or even an auntie or an uncle.

The same goes when many people tend to say that they want to be in love or they want to be loved rather in a relationship, husbands and wives, boyfriend and girlfriend, sister and brother, son's and daughter's, mother's and father's and Pastor's and members.

The problem with this word Love is we have a false sense of what love is. Love isn't you telling a person you love them, but you never show any signs of love. Love isn't you cheating on your spouse or gossiping about someone behind their backs. Love is when you look beyond the person issues and faults, and you hold on to them and show them that in spite of the things that has happened or what others may have done to them you're going to stay right there by their side.

The shortage of love comes from not dealing with the issues that stop us from loving others. The key word is Forgiveness- forgiving those who has hurt you in past relationships, Friendships, experiences, and manipulations. The reason you have to deal with the old issues is because you can't have a future without dealing with your past. Deal with everything that comes your way. Deal with the loss of a loved one, deal with the people hurting you, deal with fact that your spouse may have cheated on you, deal with the fact that you feel alone because people may have walked away from you. You would say why would I need to deal with the issues so you won't take them into a new relationship and so that you'll be able to walk in love at all aspects of your life. Even loving those who you felt like they have hurt you.

There will be times when you feel like you're alone and everyone walked away from you or even have hurt you. What you have to do at that point is deal with the pain the emotion and the feelings you are having at that point. Most people tend to brush their feelings under a rock and believe that they are able to have a healthy life with love. Not so. In order to walk in love, be love live a life filled with love you must forgive and then do the opposite of what was done to you.

"But I say to you, love your enemies, bless those who curse you, do good to those who hate you, and pray for those who spitefully use you and persecute you."
Matthew 5:44 NKJV

CHAPTER 3
HEALING

We look for healing in a physical manner. For example if your break an arm or a leg the healing manifested would be the usage of the arm or leg without hurt.

Well, the healing from what people in the church did, what your mother did or said, what your father did or said, what people you love did or said to you can be healed as well. From others saying that you would never be anything would never go anywhere in life, you can be healed.

The bible says in Psalm 147:3 NKJV, *"He heals the brokenhearted, And binds up their wounds."* We tend to live a life full of hurt and pain and never really address the true reasons as to why you can't keep a healthy relationship. Why do you need others to validate you? Why do you get involved with married men, why can't you be alone? Why do women like being with a other women and why do men like being with other men? Never dealing with the issues head on just moving forward in a life full of misery manifesting in another way of unhealthy behavior. Most people expect to be healed from all issues over night. It doesn't work that way. You have to look at the damage that was done to you. You didn't get impacted overnight so your healing isn't going to come over night. That is a process that we must work on daily. You have to do a self-evaluation which determines what is the root cause to all of the pain and all of the things you have been feeling and going through. Once this is done, you will be able to peel back layers and years of hurt. If it is hard for you to deal with the many things that have happened to you alone, then go to your Pastor, friend or a mentor because once you begin to peel back the years of hurt you will need someone there to hold and comfort you and not judge you.

The person should be a Galatians 6:2 (NKJV) person, *"Bear one another's burdens, and so fulfill the law of*

Christ." Take the time it takes to deal with your healing and allow God to do it on his time and in his timing. Healing is an important part of your moving towards your destiny and your new place of life. You cannot take old baggage into a new place or as the bible would say Mark 2:22 (NKJV), "*And no one puts new wine into old wineskins; or else the new wine bursts the wineskins, the wine is spilled, and the wineskins are ruined. But new wine must be put into new wineskins.*"

So release and be healed...

CHAPTER 4
RECOVER

Joel 2:25 -26 (NKJV)

"So I will restore to you the years that the swarming

locust has eaten,

The crawling locust,

The consuming locust,

And the chewing locust,

My great army which I sent among you.

26 You shall eat in plenty and be satisfied,

And praise the name of the Lord your God,

Who has dealt wondrously with you;

And My people shall never be put to shame."

After you have lost loved ones, after you have lost

material things, after you have gone through the

trials and the tribulations of life and you felt like you

have nothing else to lose and nothing else can be

taken from you. God will restore. You begin to get

restored when you begin to embrace all the things

that you went through, and you have allowed God to take you through the steps of your processing. Sometimes we don't understand why we had to go through the process, but it was a good thing for you to go through it. Don't allow what happened to stop you from gaining what God wants you to have and who God wants you to be.

You will know when your restoring comes when you see God removing people away from you and bringing people around you that you would never think you would be around. When God restores, he gives you DOUBLE. He restores with greater and better. He will give you a two for one blessing. For the job where you were making barely enough, he will give you abundance. Not only that he will give you vision to work for yourself. For the vehicles, you may have lost God will give you better and greater. For the apartment, he will give you a house. If you lost a girlfriend/boyfriend, God will give you a husband or wife. The things that God has removed from you is to give you better. So embrace the people that walked away and embrace the newness in that which God is going to do in your life. To recover, you must keep moving forward and forget those things that are behind you.

If you keep moving forward, you will receive everything that you lost in abundance. The key is KEEP MOVING FORWARD...

CHAPTER 5
THE PROCESS

The process of life will never feel good or look good while you're processing. You have to learn how to recognize that with all you go through it works for our good. When people walk away, that means they weren't going with you to your next destination in life, when money fades away that means there is another source that you need to tap into, when you lose an apartment god is trying to give you a house you have to see with God's eyes.

There are words that when we are going through the process, we may never want to hear which is Get over it and Grow up.

These are essential words that you need to hear from someone that loves you to get you to go through your process. You may say that these are harsh words that will push you once you finish being upset at the person that have spoken them to you.

"Then another of His disciples said to Him, "Lord, let me first go and bury my father."
But Jesus said to him, "Follow Me, and let the dead bury their own dead." Matthew 8:21-22 (NKJV)

Jesus told the disciple that because there was a purpose he was heading to and if he would have returned home to bury his father then that would have given him several reasons as to not to move forward with his purpose.

Deal with what you need to get over. Peopled walked away from you. GET OVER IT! The lies and rumors that they started about you. GET OVER It! Not being accepted. GET OVER IT! They made you feel like you weren't worth anything and devalued you. GET OVER IT! There aren't many people patting you on your back and encouraging you GET OVER IT! Get over the abandonment, get over the hurt, get over the old things.

GROW UP! Stop allowing the ones that left you or hurt you control you by you continuing to talk about what they did or how they hurt you. Stop having temper tantrums when you don't get the attention you want from people based on the fact that you are still stuck in the same place, and they have moved on.

Stop allowing what God is using to make you, build you, grow you, strengthen you, revive you and propel you because you just refuse to grow up in your process.

The process never feels good or looks good, but it is working for your good. In order for you to see that you have to get over the old things and focus on God and who God wants you to be.

"Brethren, I do not count myself to have apprehended; but one thing I do, forgetting those things which are behind and reaching forward to

those things which are ahead, I press toward the goal for the prize of the upward call of God in Christ Jesus." Philippians 3:13-14 (NKJV)

Whatever you do, do not allow anything or anyone to hinder your process of being who God called you to be and to do that which God has called you to do. The process is worth it all because you will come out as pure gold. Learn from the mistakes, Heal from the pain, allow God to reveal himself to you and move forward. Keep moving forward and don't look back YOUR CLOSER THAN IT APPEARS MOVE FORWARD...

CHAPTER 5
MOVING FORWARD

I do not consider, brethren, that I have captured and made it my own; but one thing I do: forgetting what lies behind and straining forward to what lies ahead, I press on toward the goal to with the prize to which God in Christ Jesus is calling us upward. (amp)

You thought you made the right decisions and choices to get you to where you are, here. You forgot one thing in moving forward that you have to forget about the past. Your past decisions, your past mistakes, your past choices, your past failures in relationships, money, jobs, whatever you feel like you've done wrong.

Part of moving forward is after you have gone through the healing and after you have decided to forgive those that have hurt you and after you have made up in your mind to be better. The most important thing for you to do is never return to the place you worked hard at getting out of.

You may have been in a relationship and felt like he/she was the love of your life but in that relationship, you were the one getting hurt the most or you were the one not reaping in true benefits. So God finally separated you from the person. You may have gotten lonely or you may miss the person because they keep trying to come back into your life. Don't go back to what hurt you or caused you more pain than happiness. If you focus on what you really want out of love and what you want from a relationship, you will see that God has that perfect relationship for you. Move forward and in that you maybe at a grocery store, restaurant, a gas station, at work and that person that God has for you will walk up to you and show you how love is supposed to be.

Take that same point of view on every area of your life. Nothing can consume you unless you allow it to. Change your thoughts and what you think about. Be so focused on your present and your future to where the thoughts of the past have no way of entering into your mind. If you focus meaning be fixed on conquering unforeseen events successfully you will end up in the place that God has for you. You will be who God called you to be. You will have the things that God has for you. You will pursue every dream. My daughter has a Disney movie that she likes to watch, and it's Finding Nemo there is a part in the movie where Nemo gets taken, and his father begins to look for him well in his search he runs into Dorie. We'll while they are looking for Nemo his father gets discouraged and Dorie begins to sing a song. Just keep swimming just keep swimming, swimming, swimming, swimming, swimming. That's what you have to do take on that mentality. Keep looking forward and never look backward. You look backward to see your growth and to see where you came from.

You have to ask yourself what's more important moving forward or staying in a place that you never belonged.

> **Carpe diem**
> *"Seize the moment"*

"Go, eat your bread with joy,
And drink your wine with a merry heart;
For God has already accepted your works.
Let your garments always be white,
And let your head lack no oil.
Live joyfully with the wife whom you love all the
days of your vain life which He has given you under
the sun, all your days of vanity; for that isyour
portion in life, and in the labor which you perform
under the sun." Ecclesiastes 9:7:9 (NKJV)

Enjoy life no matter what may come your way. Live your life to the fullest no matter what may come your way. Explore new places, new restaurants, explore new avenues. Live like never before. Don't let life control you, you control your life. Meaning if God allows you to see another day, live. Stop waiting on people or a man, stop sitting in the house saying that you aren't able to do the things that you desire to do because you have no money or you have no means. Start doing things that doesn't cost as much, research, plan, and conqueror.

Go to the beach, take hikes, go to different states, visit different places that you could only imagine. Live outside of your box. Explore new avenues and new ventures. Part of living is doing different things stop putting your life on hold for others before you decide to live. In seizing every moment of your life, live, be happy, make changes, go alone sometimes…. Don't let fear or doubt stop you to where you believe you can't do things by yourself that isn't true you can live and be happy alone. What are you waiting for go, make the plans to go on your trip to Jamaica, make plans to go to the beach or on a cruise So when the promised person comes they will add to your adventure to your life. Never stop living and dreaming. Live your life to the fullest.

"The purpose of life is to live it, to taste experience to the utmost, to reach out ...Love everyone and nothing at the same time. Eleanor Roosevelt

About the Author

LaTeehah Linton is the president and founder of LDL Enterprise along with Bless'sed Beauty Collections and I am a Lady First.

LaTeehah also is the Founder of the Non-Profit Organization Daughter's of Zion, Co-Founder of III Triumphant Kings.

When she is not hard at work, LaTeehah resides in Atlanta, Georgia with her family. She enjoys spending time with her five children. Laughing, dancing ,talking and taking family trips.

The most important thing to LaTeehah is to touch the lives of everyone that she encounters. Her desire is to reach young girls and help them make decisions that will change them for the betterment of themselves and their families. She strives to draw people closer to God by giving her testimony and expressions of love through her actions and giving of herself.